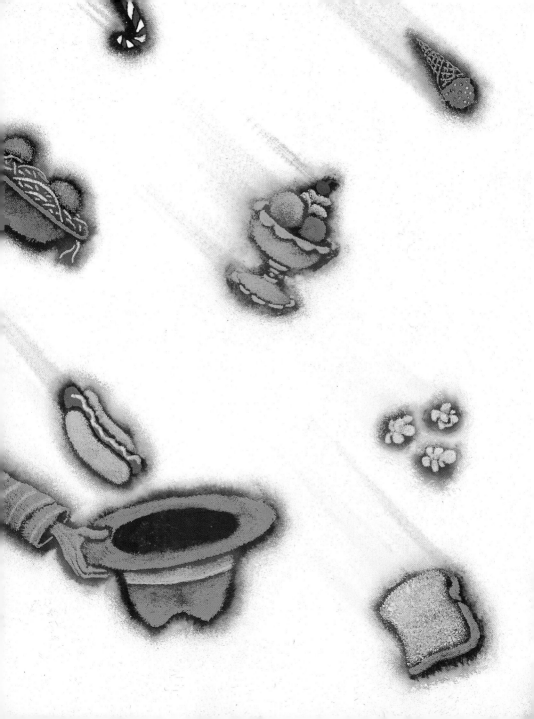

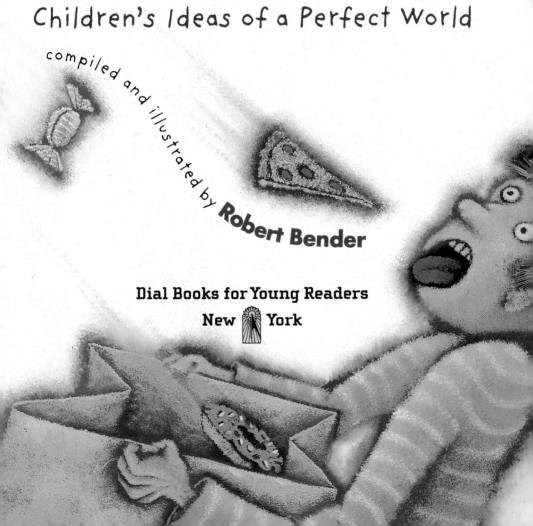

lima beans would be illegal

Children's Ideas of a Perfect World

compiled and illustrated by **Robert Bender**

Dial Books for Young Readers
New York

Dedicated to all the children who showed me
what a perfect world might be. And for
Christina . . . my partner in crime

Published by Dial Books for Young Readers
A division of Penguin Putnam Inc.
345 Hudson Street
New York, New York 10014

Printed in Hong Kong on acid-free paper
10 9 8 7 6 5 4 3 2 1

Library of Congress Cataloging in Publication Data

Lima beans would be illegal: children's ideas of a perfect world/
compiled and illustrated by Robert Bender.
p. cm.
Summary: Quotes from children stating how they
would like the world to be.
ISBN 0-8037-2532-9 (hc. trade)
1. Children—Quotations—Juvenile literature.
2. Perfection—Quotations, maxims, etc.—Juvenile literature.
3. Utopias—Quotations, maxims, etc.—Juvenile literature. [1. Quotations.]
I. Bender, Robert. II. Title: children's ideas of a perfect world.
PN6328.C5L45 2000   305.23—dc21 99-32171   CIP

The art was created using cell-vinyl paint on layers of acetate.

One of the best parts of my job as a writer and artist is that I get to visit schools. When I do, I often end up learning as much about kids as they do about me! Here are some of the things I've learned about kids:

They are very honest.

They are smart.

They have good ideas.

They like to have fun.

Thinking about all the things kids have taught me, I started to wonder if there was some way to make a book that would demonstrate all these great kid-qualities. After much brainstorming, and a little head scratching, I came up with a concept that intrigued me and that I thought would stimulate kids' imaginations as well.

To get things started, I made a list of my thoughts on what a perfect world might be like. I came up with things such as being able to bottle happy moments for later use, and having all diseases cured by spending a day at the beach. I sent my list to kids at lots of schools—some that I had visited—and asked them to write down their own ideas. It wasn't long before my mailbox began to get very, *very* full. I received thousands of quotes from children all over the country.

It turns out that a lot of kids want the same things: to have endless candy, to switch places with parents and teachers, to be able to visit with loved ones who've died. Some kids envisioned very particular things: riding on dinosaurs, having pets do their homework, and getting rid of cheese! But what the over one hundred quotes featured in these pages show most clearly is that, whether you're 6 or 36, for most of us a perfect world would be one where everyone's hopes and expectations are allowed to come true, even if only in our imaginations and dreams—and with or without lima beans!

—*Robert Bender*

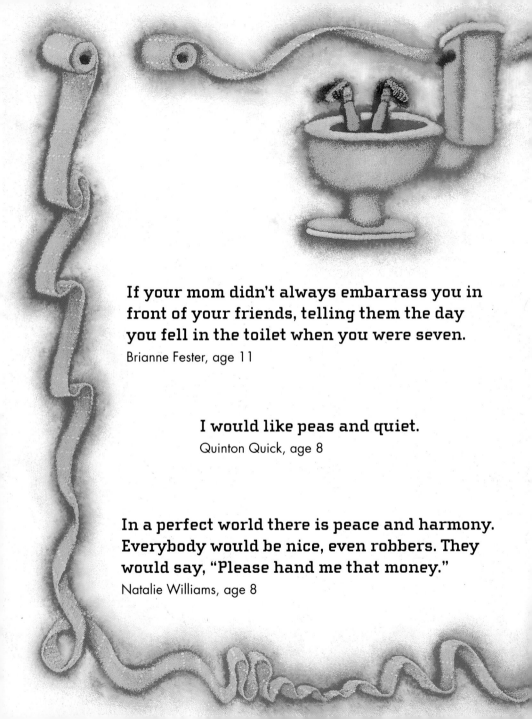

If your mom didn't always embarrass you in front of your friends, telling them the day you fell in the toilet when you were seven.

Brianne Fester, age 11

I would like peas and quiet.

Quinton Quick, age 8

In a perfect world there is peace and harmony. Everybody would be nice, even robbers. They would say, "Please hand me that money."

Natalie Williams, age 8

It would be a perfect world if you had a remote that had the buttons "off," "pause," "mute," and "on," and it worked on people. For example, if your mom told you to clean your room, you could press a button and mute her.

Chad McGrath, age 10

In a perfect world Eliza would love me, and this came true this year because she kissed me on the cheek.

Nicholas Opaliski, age 7

Heaven on earth would be if animals were potty trained.

Joshua Becker, age 7

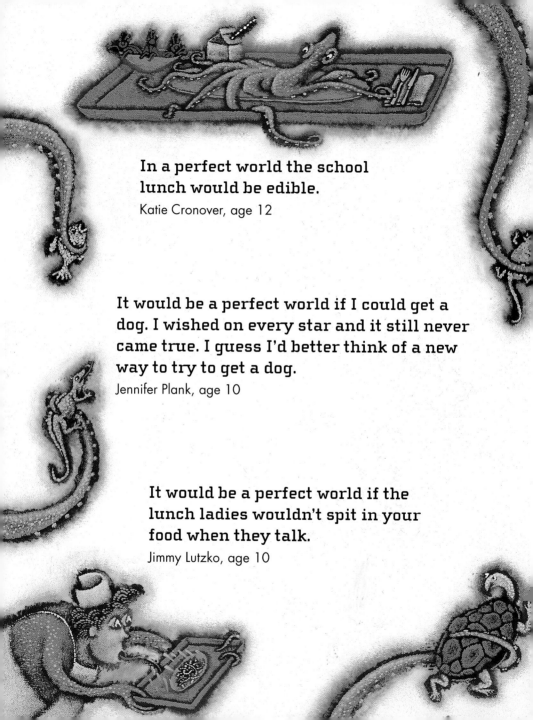

In a perfect world the school
lunch would be edible.

Katie Cronover, age 12

It would be a perfect world if I could get a
dog. I wished on every star and it still never
came true. I guess I'd better think of a new
way to try to get a dog.

Jennifer Plank, age 10

It would be a perfect world if the
lunch ladies wouldn't spit in your
food when they talk.

Jimmy Lutzko, age 10

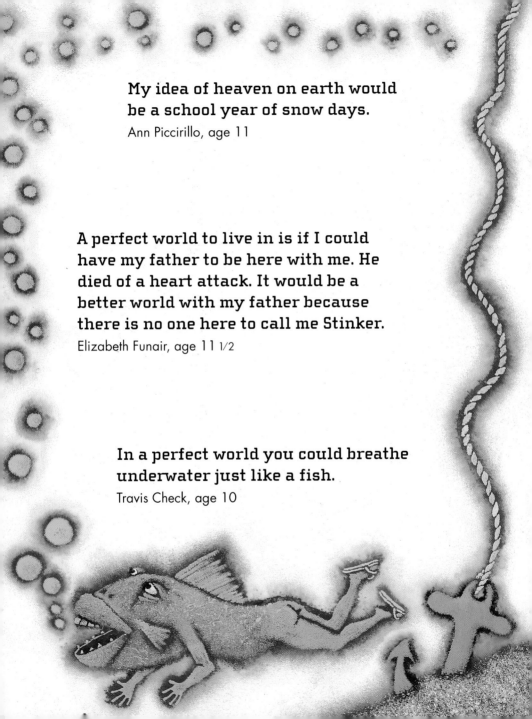

My idea of heaven on earth would
be a school year of snow days.

Ann Piccirillo, age 11

A perfect world to live in is if I could
have my father to be here with me. He
died of a heart attack. It would be a
better world with my father because
there is no one here to call me Stinker.

Elizabeth Funair, age 11 1/2

In a perfect world you could breathe
underwater just like a fish.

Travis Check, age 10

In a perfect world people would be covered in fur instead of clothes, because clothes can be a hassle.

Roberta Schettig, age 13

My idea of a perfect world is toilets installed into recliner chairs so you never have to get up and move to the bathroom. It would also have wheels on the bottom so when I had to go to the refrigerator, I could just wheel myself over there and pull out what I need.

Matt Stone, age 12

My idea of a perfect world would have no big smooches from Aunt Edna.

Brian Todd, age 11

In a perfect world I wish that my science and health teacher would stop singing every day during class time.

Danielle Hoke, age 10

The perfect world would be to find a cure for diabetes, because I would love to live like a normal person again. It would be great to do that even if it was just for one day. I would be so happy.

Bonnie Gier, age 10

I think the world would be perfect if we could talk to the animals. See how they feel about us destroying their homes. If we were them, how would we feel?

Ashley Shirk, age 9

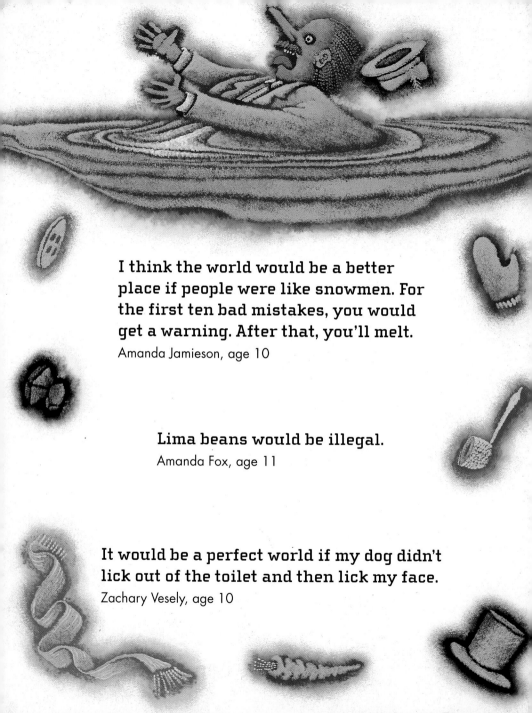

I think the world would be a better place if people were like snowmen. For the first ten bad mistakes, you would get a warning. After that, you'll melt.

Amanda Jamieson, age 10

Lima beans would be illegal.

Amanda Fox, age 11

It would be a perfect world if my dog didn't lick out of the toilet and then lick my face.

Zachary Vesely, age 10

It would be a perfect world if there wouldn't have to be an endangered species list.

Cristina Cooper, age 10

In a perfect world I would never have cancer. I would be a normal child.

Heather Barrett, age 10

In a perfect world we could bring back the dinosaurs. But we could get extincted in the process.

Zach Petak, age 11

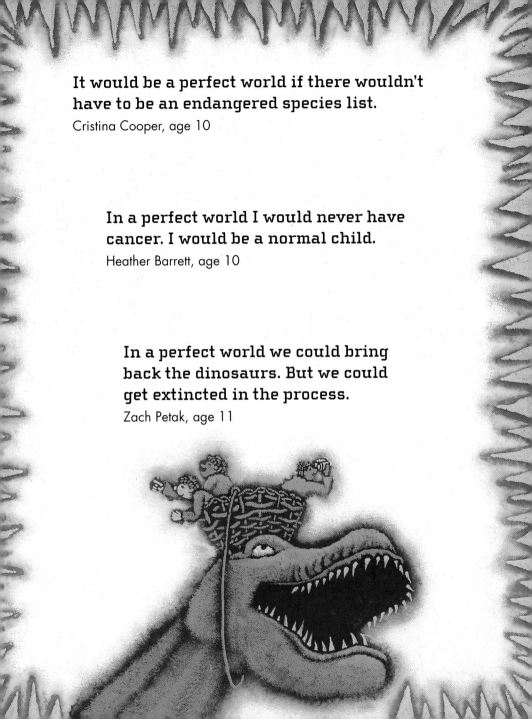

In a perfect world pumpkins would be carved big enough for houses for the poor.

Ashley Nicole George, age 9

It would be a perfect world if my friends wouldn't talk about their barf stories while I'm eating.

John Zaccaro, age 10

To me the perfect world would be having a famous celebrity as a sibling, because then you might go to one of his or her acts. And maybe they will see you doing a little bit of acting and choose you to do the show! Then you would get popular.

Courtney Landis, age 11

In a perfect world when you die and go to heaven, you can come back to earth when you get bored.

Kimberly Martel, age 7

In a perfect world there would be no cheese, because it really smells and it's too mushy, plus I hate its color.

Tyler Shuey, age 9 1/2

In a perfect world there would be everlasting cheese! Everybody likes cheese! Velveeta is my favorite!

Jeff Reitz, age 10 1/2

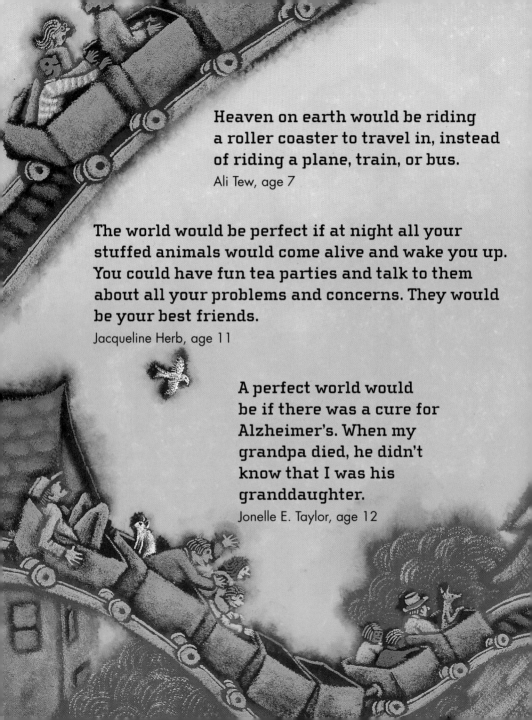

Heaven on earth would be riding a roller coaster to travel in, instead of riding a plane, train, or bus.

Ali Tew, age 7

The world would be perfect if at night all your stuffed animals would come alive and wake you up. You could have fun tea parties and talk to them about all your problems and concerns. They would be your best friends.

Jacqueline Herb, age 11

A perfect world would be if there was a cure for Alzheimer's. When my grandpa died, he didn't know that I was his granddaughter.

Jonelle E. Taylor, age 12

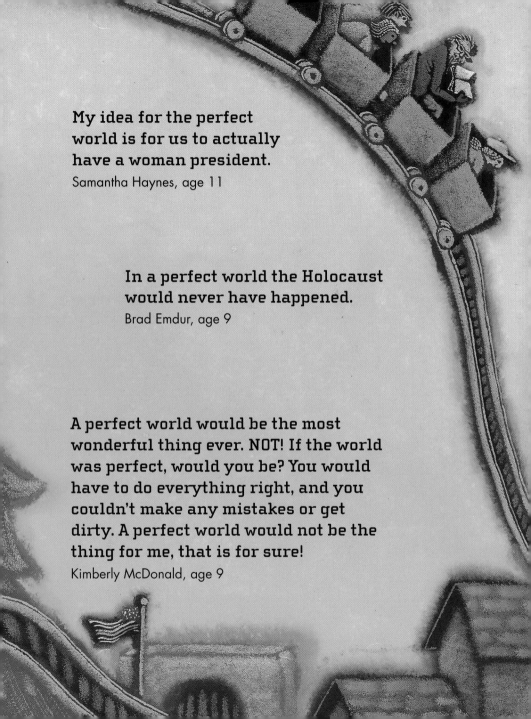

My idea for the perfect
world is for us to actually
have a woman president.

Samantha Haynes, age 11

In a perfect world the Holocaust
would never have happened.

Brad Emdur, age 9

A perfect world would be the most
wonderful thing ever. NOT! If the world
was perfect, would you be? You would
have to do everything right, and you
couldn't make any mistakes or get
dirty. A perfect world would not be the
thing for me, that is for sure!

Kimberly McDonald, age 9

In a perfect world my mom
and sister would not show my
friends my baby pictures, even
though I'm extremely cute.

Tyler Gross, age 11

In a perfect world homework would be made
of Milk Bones. Then we'd be telling the truth
when we said, "My dog ate my homework."

Max Orenstein, age 10

It would be a perfect world if your birthday
was every day. The only problem is that you
would be 365 1/4 in one year. That's old!

Julie Henninger, age 11

In a perfect world my mom wouldn't be so weird and wave to people she doesn't know.

Melissa Murray, age 12

I think a perfect world would be that all people could get along, even my brother and me. I know that will never happen. No power could get my brother to get along with me. It is impossible, but can't a little brother dream?

Charlie Bullock, age 11

In a perfect world there would be no crying baby cousins.

Stephanie Vicary, age 7

In a perfect world animals could
turn invisible to hide from hunters.

Theresa Simcic, age 11

I think the perfect world would be if
people didn't care about other people's
color. We're all in this together.

Amy Leiby, age 11

In the perfect world my grandfather
would be alive. Grandfather, I miss you
and I hope you hear me. I love you.

Patricia Marko, age 8

The world is already perfect because I got a sister and even better, she's adopted.

Nick Ott, age 11

In a perfect world you could be able to fast-forward the day or rewind the day like on a remote control. For example, if you wanted to get the day over with you just push "fast-forward."

Craig Gillmeyer, age 10

In a perfect world trash would take itself out to the curb.

Charlotte Myers, age 10

Heaven on earth would be like having
Grandma coming down to earth.

Darci Wonsettler, age 8

Heaven on earth to me is if the world was upside
down so we would have to walk on the sky.

Sharmi Elamin, age 9

All the good people that were dead came and
lived on this earth again, like my pop-pop
Christy. The bad people would stay dead.

Meghan Christy, age 11

The world would be perfect if the clouds were marshmallows and you could fly up and eat them.

Lizzie Sovia, age 11

Heaven on earth would be like if my cousin came down from heaven. I know God is keeping him warm and gives you what you want. I loved when my cousin lived in Mount Holly. I love you. By Henry to you.

Henry Pratt, age 11

My idea of a perfect world is if you can write letters to God and there would be a heaven mailman to deliver them.

Robert Carpenter, age 9

Heaven on earth would be if my puppy was an angel. But he's too fat and he's too lazy, and he doesn't listen to me, but he will bite me—but not robbers.

Desiré Jones, age 9

It would be a perfect world if every time your big brother passed gas on top of your head you had a special spray to get rid of him and his gas.

Katey De Iaco, age 11

It would be a perfect world if everybody laughed at my lame jokes.

Steven Gable, Jr., age 10

I think in a perfect world people on TV can come out of the screen. For example, if a pizza maker came out of the TV, he can make you a pizza every day.

Vincent Miller, age 9

The world would be perfect if my 14-year-old dog (98 in human years) could get up the stairs and run again, because she has doggy arthritis.

Carlyn Friedberg, age 11

In a perfect world, school bullies would wear dresses.

Staci Weidner, age 11

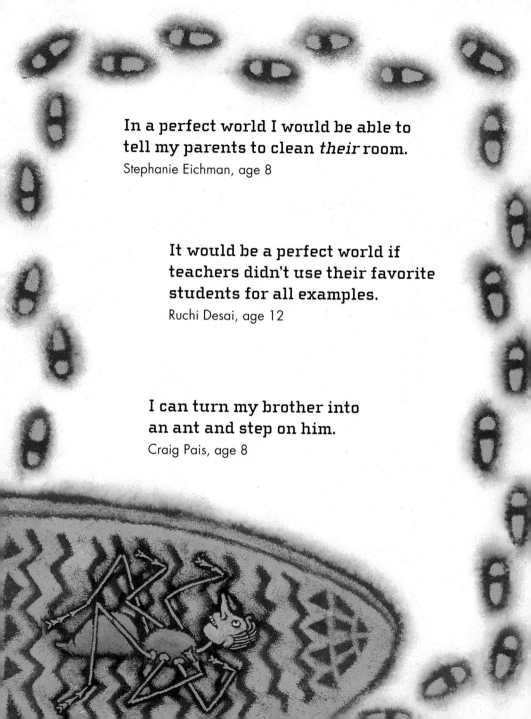

In a perfect world I would be able to tell my parents to clean *their* room.

Stephanie Eichman, age 8

It would be a perfect world if teachers didn't use their favorite students for all examples.

Ruchi Desai, age 12

I can turn my brother into an ant and step on him.

Craig Pais, age 8

In a perfect world you can have an automatic animal cleaner. But for cats you have to have a dry cleaner.

Mark Lenguarsky, age 9

A perfect world would be if you could relive a famous American's childhood and know every detail of the things they accomplished.

John Dixon, age 9

In a perfect world parents would not get divorced. My parents are divorced. I get extra love and attention this way, but I'd like them to be married.

Sarah Penich, age 9

Your pets could talk and help
you with your homework.
Aaron Ireland, age 9

A perfect world would be full of peace and
happiness, love, and NO hate!!!! But most of
all letting kids do whatever they wanted.
(Joke—don't worry, that won't happen.)
Orli Levine, age 7 1/2 and a couple of weeks

I wish that Pooh was real and he
would come and play with me and
show me where all the honey is.
Tiffani Shull, age 8

In a perfect world I wish I was Dracula and I would suck blood. I would give it to the hospitals and some people might feel better.

Samuel Bryant, age 9

That people wouldn't care about winning all the time.

Christian Reed, age 7

You could look through the holes in the floor of the sky and see all of the planets and see if there really are aliens among us.

Samantha Jo Keiser, age 9

If the world was perfect I would be happy
because then I would get to see my mom,
Carol . . . who is in heaven right now.

Lizzy Davis, age 9

In a perfect world your sister would
stay out of your diary.

Aubrie Smith, age 11

The world would be
perfect if photosynthesis
worked in people, to
prevent hunger.

Jeremy Shoup, age 12

A perfect world would be if books could read to you.

Brian Hinz, age 9

The world would be perfect if my grandpa would quit having spells.

Ryan Casassa, age 8

No little brothers that run around in circles screaming, shooting you in the head with Nerf guns.

Ryan Palm, age 11

In a perfect world you would have an extra family member just in case you can't get a ride somewhere on Friday night.

Jennifer Underhill, age 11

If your body had built-in pockets. This way you would never forget your money or your keys.

Samantha Weirman, age 9

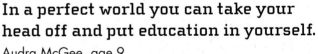

In a perfect world you can take your head off and put education in yourself.

Audra McGee, age 9

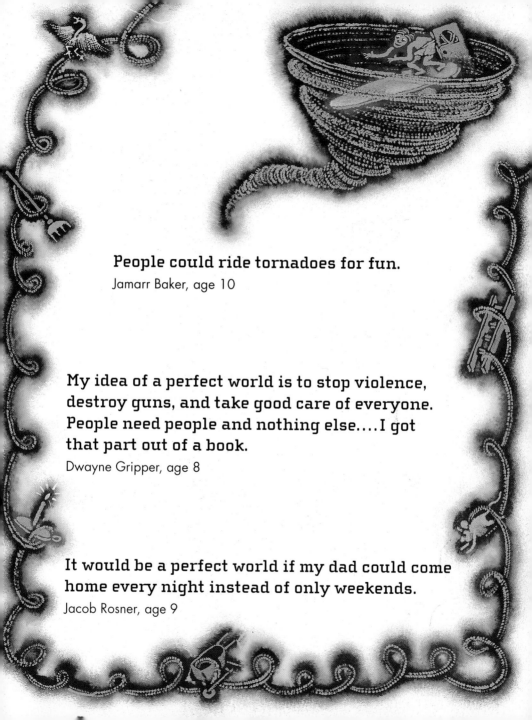

People could ride tornadoes for fun.

Jamarr Baker, age 10

My idea of a perfect world is to stop violence, destroy guns, and take good care of everyone. People need people and nothing else....I got that part out of a book.

Dwayne Gripper, age 8

It would be a perfect world if my dad could come home every night instead of only weekends.

Jacob Rosner, age 9

In a perfect world it would rain breakfast, lunch, dinner, and dessert every day. When it does rain food, all you have to do is go outside with plates, bowls, and silverware.

Lee Anne Pontzer, age 10

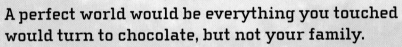

A perfect world would be everything you touched would turn to chocolate, but not your family.

Chad Walter, age 11

My idea is having a chocolate world. I would eat my brother and my worst enemies and my school.

Steven La Marco, age 8

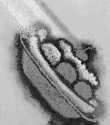

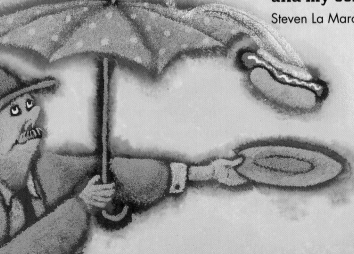

In a perfect world moms and dads would not borrow your money.

Emily Newman, age 10

There would be a machine in every house that would control the weather in your own backyard.

Nathaniel Wade, age 11

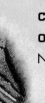

In a perfect world my sister wouldn't act so much like a monkey. She is so hyper. I wish she would act like a normal sister. Is there such a thing?

Emily Hamman, age 11

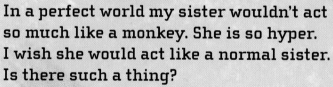

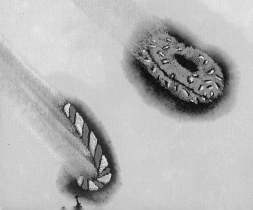

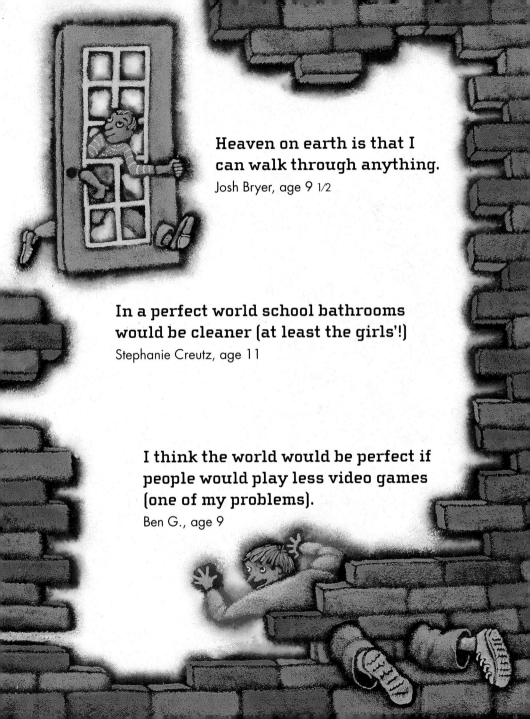

Heaven on earth is that I can walk through anything.
Josh Bryer, age 9 1/2

In a perfect world school bathrooms would be cleaner (at least the girls'!)
Stephanie Creutz, age 11

I think the world would be perfect if people would play less video games (one of my problems).
Ben G., age 9

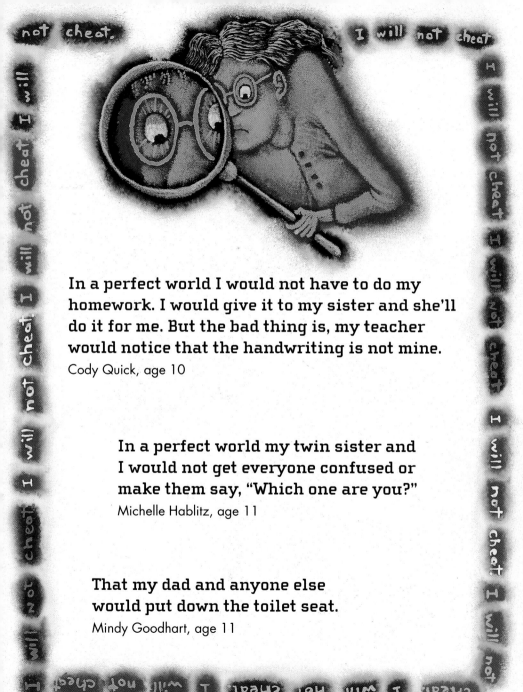

In a perfect world I would not have to do my homework. I would give it to my sister and she'll do it for me. But the bad thing is, my teacher would notice that the handwriting is not mine.

Cody Quick, age 10

In a perfect world my twin sister and I would not get everyone confused or make them say, "Which one are you?"

Michelle Hablitz, age 11

That my dad and anyone else would put down the toilet seat.

Mindy Goodhart, age 11

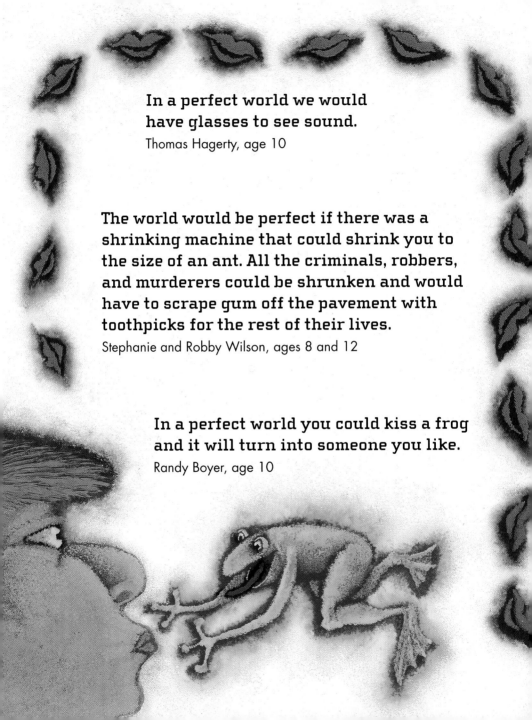

In a perfect world we would
have glasses to see sound.

Thomas Hagerty, age 10

The world would be perfect if there was a
shrinking machine that could shrink you to
the size of an ant. All the criminals, robbers,
and murderers could be shrunken and would
have to scrape gum off the pavement with
toothpicks for the rest of their lives.

Stephanie and Robby Wilson, ages 8 and 12

In a perfect world you could kiss a frog
and it will turn into someone you like.

Randy Boyer, age 10

It would be a perfect world if my mom would finally realize that I'm *never* going to clean my room.

Jimmy Lutzko, age 10

In a perfect world you can cut off part of your body and it will grow back.

Tim Pitts, age 10

No one would have bad hair days.

Anna Oliveros, age 11, and
Courtney Stewart, age 11

A perfect world would be if toys grew from the ground.

Brent Troy, age 8

I think heaven on earth would be if Ashley stopped talking about her pet hamster, Pumkin.

Adam Gollatz, age 10

I think heaven on earth would be if my hamster, Pumkin, could talk to me!

Ashley Guida, age 10

If everybody would be nice and share, even if it's not Christmas.

Curtis Barbour, age 6

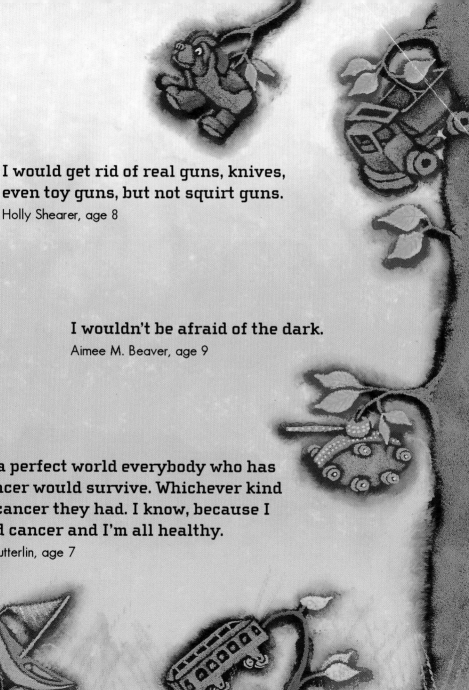

I would get rid of real guns, knives, even toy guns, but not squirt guns.

Holly Shearer, age 8

I wouldn't be afraid of the dark.

Aimee M. Beaver, age 9

In a perfect world everybody who has cancer would survive. Whichever kind of cancer they had. I know, because I had cancer and I'm all healthy.

Al Sutterlin, age 7

If your bathing suit wouldn't fall off in the pool.

David Libert, age 8

Instead of smoke coming out of the cars, it should be flowers.

Dorothy Schoellkopf, age 10

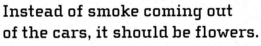

In a perfect world parents would understand and they would let you have time to explain what happened.

Jennifer Sheffler, age 10 1/2

**Everyone would have flying shoes
to zoom around. They would never
get smelly or have holes in them.**

Tyler Williams, age 6

If people never had to say good-bye.

Emily McNaughton, age 11

**If when you grew up, you could have
as much fun as when you were a kid.**

Robert Bender, age 36